THE TIME TRAP

LEO P. KELLEY

A PACEMAKER® BOOK

GLOBE FEARON

Pearson Learning Group

The PACEMAKER BESTELLERS

Bestellers I

Diamonds in the Dirt
Night of the Kachina
The Verlaine Crossing
Silvabamba
The Money Game

Flight to Fear
The Time Trap
The Candy Man
Three Mile House
Dream of the Dead

Bestellers II

Black Beach
Crash Dive
Wind Over Stonehenge
Gypsy
Escape from Tomorrow

The Demeter Star
North to Oak Island
So Wild a Dream
Wet Fire
Tiger, Lion, Hawk

Bestellers III

Star Gold
Bad Moon
Jungle Jenny
Secret Spy
Little Big Top

The Animals
Counterfeit!
Night of Fire and Blood
Village of Vampires
I Died Here

Bestellers IV

Dares
Welcome to Skull Canyon
Blackbeard's Medal
Time's Reach
Trouble at Catskill Creek

The Cardiff Hill Mystery
Tomorrow's Child
Hong Kong Heat
Follow the Whales
A Changed Man

Series Director: Tom Belina

Designer: Richard Kharibian

Cover and Illustrations: David Grove

ISBN 0-8224-5253-7

Printed in the United States of America

10 11 12 13 14   08 07 06 05 04

Globe
Fearon

Pearson Learning Group

1-800-321-3106
www.pearsonlearning.com

CONTENTS

CHAPTER 1
A NEW PARTNER

Jeff Adams was all alone on Planet X–12. He had been alone ever since his partner had become sick and returned to Earth.

As Jeff stood outside his base camp building, he kept looking up at the sky. At last, he saw what he had been watching for.

A spaceship flew into sight. It looked like another bright star in the night sky above Planet X–12.

As Jeff watched, it came closer and closer. Minutes later, it cut its jets and landed.

Jeff ran to it. Soon, he knew, he would meet his new partner who had come on the ship.

A door in the side of the ship opened. A girl stepped out. She walked toward Jeff as the door closed behind her.

"Hello," she said. "My name is Maria West." She held out her hand to Jeff.

Jeff took her hand and shook it. At first, he couldn't speak. But finally he found his voice. "You're not—I mean are *you* my new partner?"

Maria smiled. "You didn't expect a girl, did you?"

Jeff shook his head. "No, I didn't."

"I hope you don't mind. I'm one of ten girls in the Time Travel Study Group. But this is the first real job I've had since I finished school."

Did he mind, Jeff wondered. Yes, he did. He had never worked with a girl in the Time Travel Study Group before. He didn't want to work with one now. His job was hard. Sometimes it was full of danger. This girl might get hurt. But she wasn't bad-looking. She wasn't really beautiful, but she *was* pretty.

"Welcome to Planet X–12," Jeff said. "Come on inside and have a look around."

Jeff and Maria walked toward the base camp building. They didn't see a second smaller door open in the spaceship. They didn't see a man leave the spaceship and run away in the dark behind them.

Once inside the square building, Jeff showed Maria where her room was. He also showed her the tiny kitchen where they would cook their

meals. Then he showed her the notes he had
been keeping of his travels back in time.

"How far back do you—do *we*—go?" Maria
asked him.

"Three hundred years," Jeff answered. "To the time when this planet still had life on it. Of course, all the people and animals are dead now. They were all killed by insects. We don't know for sure when that happened."

"So now when we go back in time the people and animals will still be alive. Just as they were then. I mean before the insects killed them all."

"That's right," Jeff said.

"And our job is to go back and take pictures of the way life was on this planet."

"Yes. So that people on Earth can study the pictures we take. In that way they can learn what life was like here a long time ago."

"It sounds like it might be fun," Maria said.

"It's not fun. It's a job. And there can be danger. In fact, it can be very dangerous."

Maria smiled. "When do we take our first trip? I can't wait!"'

"First thing in the morning. Have you got your Timer?"

"Right here." Maria touched the little black box on her wrist. The box was small. It had three buttons on it.

"Remember this," Jeff said. "We must not do anything to change the past when we go back to it. All we must do is take pictures of how it was. If we change the past, the present will change, too. So be careful."

Maria jumped. "What was that?"

Outside the building, there was a loud noise.

"That's the spaceship," Jeff said. "It's going back to Earth."

"No, I heard another noise. Just before I heard the sound of the spaceship."

"I didn't hear anything. But I'll go out and take a look around."

Jeff went outside and walked around. When he got to the back of the base camp building, he saw a man climb out of a window.

When the man saw Jeff, he ran.

"Wait!" Jeff called out. "What are you doing? What do you want?"

But the man was gone.

Jeff looked all over for him but he couldn't find him.

He went back inside and spoke to Maria. "There was a man out there. He broke into the building. I know who he was."

"Who was he?"

"I saw his face by the light of the moon. It was Carl Kendall."

"Carl Kendall? Isn't he in jail back on Earth?"

"Not now. He's *here* now. He must have been on the ship."

"What is he doing here?" Maria asked.

"I don't know for sure. But I think I can guess. I think he's here to steal things from the past. Jewels maybe. Or other important things. The things made by the people of this planet hundreds of years ago. He can sell them for a lot of money back on Earth. I think we are in big trouble."

Maria looked at Jeff. "But he doesn't have a Timer. Without one he can't travel back into the past."

Jeff left the room. When he came back, he looked at Maria and said, "My Timer is gone. I'm sure Kendall took it when he broke in here. Now he *can* travel back in time. He can steal all he wants."

"You were right," Maria said to Jeff.

"What do you mean?"

"You were right before when you said we are in big trouble."

CHAPTER 2
BACK INTO TIME

Maria got up early the next morning. For a minute, she didn't know where she was. And then she remembered. She was on Planet X–12. She was here to travel back in time!

She got up and checked her Timer. It was in good shape. She put on her uniform.

When she came out to the kitchen, Jeff was making breakfast.

"Sit down," he said. "How do you like your eggs?"

"Over easy. Do you want me to cook them?"

"I bet you think I'll make a mess out of them. Listen, these will be the best eggs you ever ate. You'll see."

When he had given her the eggs, Maria decided that he was right. They were cooked just right.

"Would you like some more?" Jeff asked, when she had finished her eggs.

"No, thanks. That was just fine. You're a very good cook."

She helped Jeff wash the dishes.

When they had finished the dishes, he said, "Wait for me. I'll be right back." He left the kitchen.

He came back in a minute. "I had to get a new Timer out of the storeroom. It's a good thing Kendall didn't steal all the Timers we have."

Maria touched the Timer she wore on her wrist.

Jeff smiled at her. "Don't be afraid. I'll be right beside you on our trip back in time."

"I'm not afraid. Well, maybe I am—just a little bit. It's my first trip back in time."

Jeff said, "I felt the same way the first few trips. Come on. Let's get our cameras." He picked up his and gave one to Maria.

"Now," he said, "first you set your Timer for three hundred years ago. Like this." He started to show her how to do it. But Maria had already set her Timer.

"OK," he said. "Now just press your Depart Button."

As Maria pressed the Depart Button on her Timer, Jeff pressed the Depart Button on his.

They both felt a cold wind blow all around them. Then they heard a noise that was like a lot of people whispering all at once.

They felt themselves begin to move. But not in space. They were making their move in time! They could see nothing. Because now it was as black as a night without a single star in the sky.

The strange wind went on—they could hear it. The noise that was like loud whispers also went on. The space around them was all black.

And then, all at once, the whispers stopped. The wind stopped. It was not black. They could see now.

They looked around them. There were people near them. But the people did not look like humans. They had two eyes like humans. But they also had another eye just above their other two. Each of their hands had ten fingers instead of five. Their skin was as green as the sky above them.

The clothes they had on were made of gold.

"Press Button Number Two on your Timer!" Jeff said to Maria. "Quick!"

She pressed it.

"Now they can't see or hear us," he whispered. "Button Number Two changes light and sound waves. It lets us see and hear them but they can't see or hear us."

"Look!" Maria said. "Isn't that building beautiful?" She pointed to a building near them. It was tall and thin and covered with gold pictures.

"That's their art museum," Jeff said. "That's where they keep all the art they make. In there are jewels, pictures—all kinds of beautiful things."

Maria took a picture of the building. She moved to one side and took another picture.

Jeff took pictures, too.

"It's nice here," Maria said as they walked around the city.

"Yes, it is," Jeff said. "It's too bad that the insects came and killed all the people and animals. Look over there."

Maria looked where Jeff had pointed. She saw a machine fly by in the sky. It was made of glass. It had four wings that went up and down. It looked like a strange bird in the green sky.

Maria took a picture of the machine.

Jeff took a picture of a funny little animal that was near them. It was playing with its tail.

"It looks like a duck with the ears of a dog," Jeff said.

"Is it dangerous?" Maria wondered out loud.

"Some of the animals here are dangerous," Jeff said. "But that one isn't."

"I hope we don't meet any of the dangerous ones," Maria said. "I don't mind a duck that looks a little bit like a dog. But I wouldn't want to meet any dangerous animals."

Just then a big animal flew through the sky above them. They looked up at it. It looked like a giant orange lion with wings. It beat its wings against the glass machine that also flew in the sky. The machine shook.

A woman in the glass machine had a long red gun. She shot a bullet at the animal.

The animal roared and fell from the sky.

"That's the kind of animal I mean," Maria said. "I hope we don't meet any more of them."

"So do I," Jeff said.

CHAPTER 3

THE JEWELS OF PLANET X-12

Jeff and Maria walked past the body of the dead animal.

"It's the same in any place—in any time," Jeff said, looking at the dead animal. "Life is hard. People and animals have to fight to live. Some lose their fight. Some win it."

His voice sounded sad to Maria. She wondered what he was thinking about. Was he thinking about the dead animal? She waited for him to go on. But he said no more.

Suddenly, she stopped. "Oh, Jeff, look at that!" She pointed to a field that was full of flowers. It was right in front of them. "Isn't it beautiful?"

"Those flowers are special," Jeff said. "Let me show you what I mean." He went to the edge of a lake that was next to the field of flowers. He splashed water from the lake on some of the flowers.

The flowers began to sing.

Their song had no words. But it was the most beautiful song that Maria had ever heard.

She could not speak. She just stood there and listened to the yellow and blue flowers sing.

Finally, she said, "I like them better than the flowers on Earth."

"Water makes them sing," Jeff said. "You should hear them when it rains. When they are all wet—well, it's really great."

After Maria took a picture of the flowers, they walked back to the city. The song of the flowers followed them.

Once inside the city again, they went toward the museum. People passed close to them. But the people could not see or hear Jeff and Maria. This was because they had pressed Button Number Two on their Timers.

"Shall we go inside the museum?" Maria asked Jeff.

"Yes. Let's go in."

Maria went in first. Jeff followed her.

They stood and looked at the beautiful things inside the museum. Statues stood in the corners of the room. Pictures made with many colors of paint hung on the walls. The statues looked like the people of Planet X–12. The pictures were of the people and the animals that lived on the planet.

One picture became Maria's favorite almost at once. It was a picture of the field of flowers that they had just seen.

"I wish I could take that picture back with me," Maria said. "It's so very nice. I wish it were mine."

"The past must stay the way it is," Jeff said. "We must not change anything in it."

"Don't you ever want to change your own past, Jeff?" Maria asked the question because Jeff's voice sounded sad. She wondered if something in his own past had made him sad.

He looked at her. His look was not a happy one. His eyes were sad.

Maria wished that she had not asked the question.

He said, "I was very much in love with a girl once. I think she loved me, too. But her love for me didn't last. She left me."

"I'm sorry."

Jeff looked away. Maria couldn't see his face.

He said, "I guess that's why I like to travel back in time. Maybe I'm afraid to live in the present. I feel safer in the past. I guess I don't want to be hurt again."

"Sometimes love doesn't die," Maria said. "Not if it's true love. Not if two people really care about each other."

"I'd like to believe you," Jeff said.

Maria left him and walked to a far corner of the room. She looked at the statue that stood in the corner. She took several pictures of it. As she was doing so, she almost forgot where she was and about Jeff. But when she heard him shout, she ran back to him.

"What's the matter, Jeff?"

"It's Kendall!" Jeff said. "He's here!"

Maria saw that what Jeff had said was true. Carl Kendall stood across the room from them.

"Stay where you are, Kendall!" Jeff yelled. "And drop those jewels!"

Maria saw that Kendall held many jewels in his hands. She saw where they had come from. Kendall had taken them from their places in the museum.

"I have them now," Kendall said to Jeff. "And I'm going to keep them."

Jeff went to where Kendall stood. "Put them back. *Now!*"

But Kendall didn't put the jewels back. Instead, he put all of them in his pockets.

Jeff tried to grab Kendall. But Kendall jumped away. The second time Jeff tried to grab him, Kendall hit him.

Then Jeff hit Kendall. Kendall fell to the floor.

"Get up," Jeff said to him. "And drop those jewels. They belong here in the museum."

For a minute, Kendall did not move. But then, just as Jeff reached for him, he got to his feet. "You better worry about that girl over there instead of about me," Kendall said. It was a trick.

Jeff turned to see where Maria was. When he did so, Kendall grabbed a small statue and hit Jeff on the head with it.

"Jeff!" Maria called out. She ran to where he lay on the floor.

Before she could get to him, Kendall kicked Jeff on the side of the head.

"Stop it!" Maria yelled.

Kendall laughed. His laugh was an ugly sound in the air.

Maria called Jeff's name.

But he didn't answer her. His eyes were closed.

Maria looked up at Kendall.

But he was gone. And so were the jewels.

CHAPTER **4**
THE CREATURE WITH NO EYES

"Jeff!" Maria called.

He still did not answer her. His eyes were still closed. He was not moving.

What should she do? Maria wondered. Maybe she should ask the people of Planet X–12 for help. There were several people near her right now. They were looking at the pictures on the walls.

No, she knew she couldn't ask them for help. She knew she must not change the past. And she would change it if she let the people see or hear her.

Was there no one to help her, then? Was she all alone with no one at all to help her?

She faced the facts. She *was* alone. So she was the only one who could help Jeff. It was up to her.

But how? What could she do?

She remembered the lake that was next to the field of flowers. She had an idea. She ran out of the museum.

She ran to the lake. Once there, she tore a piece of cloth from her uniform. She put the cloth in the cold water of the lake. When it was all wet, she ran back to the museum with it.

She put the cold wet cloth on Jeff's head. She rubbed his wrists.

Jeff moved a little bit.

Maria rubbed his wrists some more. "Jeff? It's me. It's Maria. Jeff?"

He opened his eyes. "Maria?"

"Yes, I'm here. Are you OK now?"

"What happened to me?"

Maria told Jeff how Kendall had hit him on the head with a statue.

"I remember now," he said. He put his hand to his head. He took the wet cloth from it. "Thanks, Maria," he said. "Thanks a lot for your help."

"I think we had better go back now to our own time," Maria said.

"You're right." Jeff stood up. He almost fell down again.

Maria put her arm around him. Together they left the museum.

"Sit down here on this rock," Maria said. "You'll be OK in a minute. I'll go and get some more cold water."

She ran to the lake and wet the piece of cloth. But when she came back to where she had left Jeff, he was gone.

She looked around. He was not in sight. "Jeff," she called. "Where are you?"

He must have been hurt worse than he knew, Maria decided. He probably just walked away. He probably didn't know what he was doing.

Maria began to look for him. But she couldn't find him. She called his name several times.

She walked along beside the lake. She went to the field of flowers. The flowers were not singing now. All was quiet.

She was almost ready to give up when she heard Jeff call her name.

"I'm here, Jeff," she called back. "Where are you?" There was no sign of him.

"Over here, Maria! *Help me!*"

She ran toward the sound of Jeff's voice. She found him near some trees beside the lake. She could not believe what she saw.

A giant creature had caught Jeff! It had hundreds of long thin legs. Its body was a big blue ball. It did not seem to have any eyes.

It was making a web. The web was like the kind made by spiders back on Earth. But it was much stronger. And it was much bigger.

Jeff was caught in the web. He couldn't free himself.

"Stay back, Maria," Jeff called out to her. "The creature might get you, too!"

Maria could not move. She didn't know what to do. The ugly creature went on making the web in which it had caught Jeff.

Maria knew that she had to act. She couldn't just stand and watch. If she did, the creature was sure to kill Jeff.

But what could she do? She didn't know. She looked around her.

"Maria," Jeff yelled. "Get a big stick. Get one that's sharp. . . ."

Maria ran to a tree near her. She reached up and broke off a branch of the tree. Now she knew what to do. But could she do it? She wasn't at all sure that she could. But she would try. She would have to try. If she didn't try. . . . She wouldn't let herself think of what might happen if she didn't try to save Jeff.

She came close to the web the creature had made. But she did not come too close. If the creature caught her, she would die along with Jeff. Her heart was pounding.

Suddenly one of the creature's legs grabbed for Maria. She didn't see it until it was almost too late. She jumped back just as the creature's leg touched her.

Now two more of the creature's long, thin legs came at her.

"Look out!" shouted Jeff. He was fighting to get free of the creature's web. But he could not break free.

Maria jumped out of the way again. She felt like she was going to be sick. She wanted to run. But she knew she could not. She had to stay and try to save Jeff.

Maria knew what she had to do. She got a good hold on the stick and rushed toward the creature.

"Be careful!" Jeff told her. He couldn't speak very well now. The web had almost closed his mouth.

Maria hit the creature with the stick. She hit it again. She hit it a third time.

Its hundreds of legs reached out to grab her. One of them caught her left arm.

The creature began to pull Maria into its web, like a spider would do to a fly.

CHAPTER 5
KENDALL AGAIN

Maria could feel her heart pounding. She knew she had to do something quick.

She took the stick and hit the creature's leg that had grabbed her own arm. She broke its leg. It let her go.

Without waiting another minute, she hit the body of the creature again. Green blood spilled from the creature's body. Some of it splashed on Maria.

"Hit it again!" Jeff yelled. "Just one more hit might kill it!"

Maria hit the creature with all her might.

The creature screamed. Its legs did not move again. It hung there in the web it had made.

It was dead.

Maria dropped the stick. She began to tear at the web. She tore it to pieces. When she was finished, Jeff was free!

"Thanks again," Jeff said to her.

"Oh, it was nothing," Maria said. Her heart was still pounding. "I'm always ready for a good fight against giant creatures." She smiled.

Jeff smiled back. He knew she had saved his life. She had put herself in great danger to do it. "Are you hurt?" he asked her.

She shook her head. "Let's not stay here for even one more minute. I've had enough for one day. Let's go back where we belong."

Both of them pressed the Return Buttons on their Timers.

The wind began to blow. The whispers began again. All around them it was black.

And then, suddenly, they were back at their base camp building.

"I'm glad that is over," Maria said. She sat down on a chair.

Jeff washed the green blood of the creature from her face. "But it's *not* over," he said. "We have to go back again. It's our job. But maybe you don't want to go back. Do you?"

Maria didn't say anything right away. Then she looked up at Jeff. "You're right. It's our job. Of course we will go back. Maybe we won't meet any more creatures."

"But we might meet Carl Kendall," Jeff said.

Maria said nothing.

"He is a dangerous man," Jeff said. "Not just to us. He could make a mess back there in the past. We must get those jewels back from him. They belong in the past."

"How can we do that?"

"If we had a gun. . . ."

"We can't take a gun back there," Maria said. "You know that is against the rules of the Time Travel Study Group."

"I know. I guess we will just have to do the best we can."

Maria left the room to change her dirty uniform. When she came back, Jeff had dinner ready.

They ate it and then they both went to their rooms to sleep.

Maria was the first one to get up the next morning. She called Jeff. They put on their uniforms. Then they ate the breakfast that Maria had made for them.

"I think I made better eggs yesterday," Jeff joked.

"Maybe you did make better eggs," Maria said. "But I fight giant creatures better than you do."

"You win," Jeff said and gave a loud laugh.

Both of them put on their Timers.

"Well, here we go again," Jeff said.

Maria didn't say anything.

They pressed the Depart Buttons on their Timers.

Almost at once, they were back in the past. They stood again in front of the museum.

"Do you see any creatures?" Maria asked.

"No," Jeff said. "Not one. Maybe this time we will be in luck."

"I hope so," Maria said.

"I take back what I just said," Jeff whispered in her ear.

"What do you mean?"

"Look over there."

Maria looked and saw Carl Kendall. He was just going inside the museum.

"You stay here," Jeff told her. *"I'm* going after *that* creature. This time, it's my turn."

But Maria wouldn't let him go by himself. She went with him.

Inside the museum, they looked for Kendall. At first, they didn't see him. But then Maria spotted him.

"He's over there," she whispered to Jeff. She pointed.

Kendall was stealing more jewels from the museum.

Jeff began to move toward Kendall. He made no sound. When he got to him, he grabbed him. He held Kendall's arms behind his back.

"I've got you now," Jeff said. "I'm taking you back to the present. I'll lock you up in the storeroom. That will make a pretty good jail. Then we can ship you back to Earth—to the police."

"No, you won't!" Kendall said. He broke free and ran across the room to where Maria stood. He grabbed her.

"Now what are you going to do?" Kendall asked Jeff.

Jeff didn't move. He saw that Kendall had a gun.

While Kendall held Maria, he pointed the gun at Jeff. He was going to shoot Jeff.

"Look out, Jeff!" Maria called out.

CHAPTER **6**

TRAPPED IN TIME

"Put your hands up!" Kendall yelled.

Jeff did as he was told. Kendall was pointing the gun right at Jeff's face.

"I'm going to kill *you* first!" Kendall said. "After I kill you, I'll kill the girl!"

"You won't get away with it, Kendall," Jeff yelled back. "If you kill us, you'll get caught. The Time Travel Study Group will come looking for us. They will get you."

Kendall was about to fire.

Jeff knew it. He waited.

Just as the gun went off, Jeff threw himself to the floor.

The bullet passed over his head. At once, Jeff jumped up and ran toward Kendall.

Before Kendall could do anything to stop him, Jeff was on him. He landed on Kendall, knocking him down. Jeff hit Kendall on the arm. The gun fell to the floor.

"Get it, Maria!" Jeff yelled. "Get the gun!"

Maria grabbed the gun. "Get up, Kendall," she said. She held his gun in her hand. It was pointed at Kendall's heart. "You heard me. Get up. Get away from Jeff."

Kendall did as she told him.

"Good work," Jeff said as he joined Maria. They stood side by side in front of Kendall.

"Give me the jewels, Kendall," Jeff said. He held out his hand.

"Hand them over," Maria said, still holding the gun on him.

Kendall gave Jeff the jewels he had taken.

Jeff put them in his pocket. "Now," he said to Kendall, "all of us are going back to the base camp building. You're going into the storeroom. I'm going to lock the door on you. It's not the best jail, but it will do until we can ship you back to Earth."

Jeff turned to Maria. "Ready?"

"I'm ready," she said.

"Kendall?"

"I'll get you yet," Kendall said to Jeff. *"Both* of you."

"When I count three, press the Return Button on your Timer, Kendall," Jeff said. "Got that? You too, Maria. We're going together—the three of us. Don't try to escape, Kendall. You'll never make it."

"OK," Kendall said. "You win."

"That's better," Jeff said. Then he began to count. "One." He kept his eyes on Kendall. "Two." Maria still held the gun in her hand.

"Three," Jeff said.

But before he could press the Return Button on his Timer, Kendall knocked the gun from Maria's hand. He picked it up from the floor and fired it at Maria.

Jeff pushed her down just as the gun went off. The bullet just missed her.

Jeff made a grab for Kendall, but Kendall pressed the Return Button on his Timer and was gone.

"Well," Jeff said, "at least we have the jewels he took. Next time, we will get him, too."

"Let's go after him," Maria said. "Quick!"

"We can't," Jeff said. "We don't know where he went. He could have gone back to the base camp. Or maybe he only went an hour forward in time. Or even one hour *back* in time from here. We would never be able to find him."

"Let's take our pictures then. We might as well finish the job we came here to do."

"Good idea," Jeff said.

They took pictures of the people of Planet X–12. They took pictures of their strange houses. They took some pictures at a party that some of the people were having.

"I guess that will be enough for this trip," Jeff said a little later. "Let's go home now."

"OK," said Maria.

They got ready to leave.

"Oh, Jeff," Maria said. "Look at this." She held out her wrist to him.

"Your Timer," he said, looking at her wrist. "It's broken. How did that happen?"

"It must have happened when Kendall fired his gun at me before. He must have hit it. I didn't notice it until now."

"Here," Jeff said. He took the Timer off his wrist. "Take mine."

Maria looked at him. "We have only one Timer between us. That means that one of us is trapped in time!"

"Take it," Jeff said. "Go back. There are other Timers in the storeroom. You can get one and bring it back with you. Then we can both get out of here."

Maria shook her head. "No. I'll stay here. You go back."

"No, I won't," Jeff said. "It's too dangerous for you to stay here all alone."

"Let's not fight about it," Maria said. "I'll be OK. You go. You know where the Timers are kept in the storeroom. I don't. Maybe I wouldn't be able to find them. While you're gone, I'll put back the jewels that Kendall took."

Finally, Jeff said he would go. He gave the jewels to Maria. She gave him Kendall's gun to take back with him.

He pressed his Timer and left.

When he was gone, Maria looked around her. She hoped that Jeff would come back soon. If, for any reason, he didn't return, she would stay trapped in time. Trapped on a strange world three hundred years in the past.

CHAPTER **7**

THE ROCKSLIDE

Maria had never felt so alone in her whole life. Alone in time and space.

She could see the people of Planet X–12 all around her. But she still felt alone. Because these people were from another world. If she needed help, they couldn't help her.

The only person who could help her now was Jeff. And he was three hundred years away.

She put back the jewels that Kendall had taken. Then she went outside the museum.

She looked up at the sky. No ugly animals flew there now. There were no dangerous creatures in the streets. But where was Kendall? She couldn't help but worry about him. He might come back. If he did. . . . She didn't like to think about what might happen if he did come back.

She wanted to go back to visit the field of flowers. But she didn't go. Jeff might come back while she was gone. She had to be there when he came back for her.

She walked around the museum and looked again at the beautiful pictures on the wall. She looked at the statues. They were not a bit like pictures or statues on Earth. But they were all beautiful in their own way.

As she moved about the room, she felt sad. All the people of Planet X–12 who were in the room with her would die. So would their world. They would die when the insects came.

She wished she could save them. Or something beautiful that they had made. She wanted to remember them and their world.

She was thinking about Jeff again. What if he couldn't find a Timer in the storeroom? Would he come back here if he couldn't? Or would he have to leave her here?

He will come back, she told herself. I know I will. He has to.

She looked at a tiny picture of the museum itself. It was made of many bright colors and gold. Some of the colors she had never seen on Earth.

She wanted to take the picture. She wanted to keep it for her very own. But she did not touch it. She knew she must not change the past. Everything had to be the way it had to be.

As she turned away from the little picture, she bumped right into Carl Kendall!

He grabbed her wrists. "Don't try to escape," he told her.

But she did try, only to find that she couldn't free herself. "Let me go!" she said.

"I came for *you* this time," Kendall said. "Not the jewels. "I'll get *them* later. After I get you out of the way. You and your friend. Where is he? Tell me!"

Maria did not answer Kendall's question.

"It doesn't matter," Kendall said. "I'll find him. And when I do. . . ."

He began to laugh.

Maria knew what he would do if he found Jeff. He would kill him. Just as now, she was sure he was going to kill her.

"Come outside," Kendall said. "Don't try anything funny. I've got another gun."

When they got outside the museum, rain began to fall.

Maria broke free and started to run. She could hear Kendall running after her.

Where could she go?

To the field of flowers! She could hide there. She kept running. Kendall was still after her. She heard him fire his gun. She heard a bullet hit a tree near her.

When she reached the flowers, she jumped into the middle of them. She lay down close to the ground hoping he wouldn't see her. From where she lay, she could see him looking for her.

The rain that was falling wet the flowers. They began to sing.

Maria was glad to hear their song. Because if she moved or made a noise now, Kendall probably wouldn't be able to hear her. The song of the flowers was too loud.

"Come out!" Kendall yelled. "I won't hurt you. Don't be afraid!"

Maria knew that what he said was a lie. He *would* hurt her. He would kill her—and Jeff too—if he could. Then he could take all the jewels he wanted. There would be no one to stop him. No one at all.

The song of the flowers went on and on. But, as Maria lay among them, she heard another sound. She wasn't sure what it was. It was soft at first. But then it grew loud.

She saw the people of the planet begin to run away from the field.

Why were they running? she wondered.

And then she knew. She saw the rocks on the mountain near the field begin to fall down. They were falling toward her!

The rain had caused a rockslide!

Rocks were rolling down the mountain. Some were small. But others were as big as houses.

One of the rocks came flying down the mountain into the field of flowers. It landed very close to where Maria was hiding, smashing some of the singing flowers.

Maria knew she could not stay where she was. If she did, she would be killed by the rockslide.

But if she got up, Kendall would see her. And he had a gun.

Maria didn't know what to do. She tried to think. But she was almost too frightened to do so. Her heart was pounding. Her mouth was dry and her hands felt wet.

Another rock landed near her, smashing more of the singing flowers. The flowers cried out and died as the rock rolled over them.

More and more rocks were rolling down the mountain. The rockslide was getting worse.

Maria made up her mind. She would run for it. She had to.

She got to her feet and began to run.

Kendall saw her. "Stop!" he yelled. His voice was filled with hate.

He fired his gun. Maria heard the bullet fly by her ear. She was running as fast as she could. But it seemed to her that she was not moving at all. She seemed to be standing still.

Another bullet flew by. "Stop!" Kendall yelled again. "Stop, or I'll kill you!"

She didn't stop. She kept on running. She was almost out of the field when the rockslide caught her.

She fell down and the rocks almost completely covered her. Her body hurt all over. She couldn't move.

The rain stopped.

Kendall watched as the rockslide caught Maria and covered her with rocks. At first he thought that the rockslide had killed her. He was about to go back to the museum. He wanted to steal jewels from the museum before Jeff came back.

But then he saw something move under the rocks. It was Maria's arm. She had not been killed by the rockslide. She was still living. She was trying to free herself from the rocks that had trapped her.

But Kendall could see that she could never get free by herself. There were too many rocks. He decided to leave her where she was. He turned and walked back toward the museum.

Then he stopped. Only one of Maria's arms was free. But Kendall knew that if she could reach her other wrist with her free hand, she would be able to press the button on her Timer. If she did, she could escape the rockslide by moving into the past or the future. She could go back and get Jeff. Then the two of them would be after him again.

No, that must not happen. Kendall would not let it happen. He knew he would have to kill Maria. He checked his gun. Then he started across the field of flowers toward her.

Kendall came up to where she was trapped. He pointed his gun at her. "You're finished now!" he said.

CHAPTER **8**

ATTACK OF THE INSECTS

Back at the base camp building, Jeff took a Timer from the storeroom. He put it on his wrist. He stopped and looked around.

The building seemed empty without Maria there. He missed her. He wanted to be with her. She was, he felt, the best partner he had ever had. He liked to work with her. Together, he felt, they made a good team. They helped each other. They did the job right.

But was that all? Did he like Maria just because she was a good partner? Or was there something more to it? Why did he miss her so much now? Was he falling in love with her?

One thing was sure. He felt lost without her. Maybe that *was* love. It sure was something.

He pressed the Depart Button on his Timer. He felt glad. Because he would soon be with Maria again.

When he got back to the past, he didn't see her. Where was she? He looked all over for her. She wasn't in the museum. Maybe she was taking pictures outside.

Jeff searched the city but he couldn't find her. He began to worry about Maria. He went to the field of flowers but he couldn't find her there, either. And she wasn't at the lake.

He was about to go back to the city when he saw a crowd of people. They were looking at something. He joined the crowd.

When he did, he saw the rockslide. He also saw Maria and Kendall. The people of Planet X–12 could see only the rockslide. They couldn't see or hear Maria or Kendall or Jeff.

"Kendall!" Jeff yelled. "Don't shoot her!"

Kendall turned toward him. "So you're back, are you? Good. Now I can take care of both of you at the same time. Get over here. Move! If you don't, I'll shoot Maria right now."

Jeff went over to Maria. She was still caught in the rockslide and couldn't move.

"Jeff," she said, "I'm sorry. I should have been more careful. I shouldn't have let Kendall catch me."

"Don't worry about it now," Jeff said to her.

"You better worry about it," Kendall said. "Both of you better worry a whole lot. Because I'm going to put both of you out of my way for good."

He took a step closer to them. The gun in his hand moved a little.

Jeff tried to help Maria. He started pulling the rocks away from her.

"Don't move!" Kendall yelled.

"But I've got to help her," Jeff said. "Just let me . . ."

"No!" Kendall yelled. "Get away from her. I know you two and your tricks!"

Kendall didn't see the rock in Jeff's hand. He was hiding it behind his back. Suddenly, he turned and threw it at Kendall.

The rock hit him in the face. He let out a yell and fell over. The rock had knocked him out.

Jeff turned back to Maria. He gave her Kendall's gun. "You hold on to it while I free you from these rocks."

Soon he had freed Maria. He helped her get to her feet.

"What do we do now?" she asked.

"I'm going to take Kendall back with me."

"To the base camp?"

"Yes," Jeff answered. "You stay here. I don't think you'll have any trouble after I've taken Kendall away."

Jeff went over to Kendall. He was going to press the Return Button on Kendall's Timer. At the same time, he would press the Return Button on his own Timer. When he had done so, they would both return to the base camp. He would put Kendall in the storeroom—in jail.

But before he could do anything, Kendall's eyes opened. He pushed Jeff away from him and ran toward Maria. "I'll kill you if it's the last thing I ever do," Kendall yelled.

Maria remembered the rules of the Time Travel Study Group. No guns. She looked at the gun she held in her hand. Rules were OK. But she would have to break the rule about guns to save herself now.

No, she couldn't. It wasn't just because there was a rule. It was because of the *reason* for the rule. If she fired the gun, she would change what happened in time. In the real past on this planet, she had not been there. There had been no gun. If she fired the gun, she would change the past. And she knew that if she did, it would change the present. That was the reason for the rule. If you change the past, you also change the present.

Kendall rushed at her. He was trying to get the gun away from her. He did not care about any rules. He did not care about the past. Only about the present—and only about himself.

Maria tried to keep him from getting the gun. But he was too strong. He started to pull it out of her hand.

Suddenly Jeff was on him. He grabbed Kendall and threw him to the ground.

But Kendall was up again in a flash. He jumped at Jeff. Jeff stepped back, but not in time. Kendall knocked him down. He hit Jeff in the face with all his might. Then he grabbed Jeff around the neck. He was going to kill him.

"Get away from him!" Maria shouted at Kendall. "Leave him alone!"

But Kendall kept on. Jeff was almost finished. His face was turning blue.

The rules! The rules! No, she could not let herself think about the rules. In another minute Jeff would be dead. Dead in the past. Dead in the present. Dead forever.

She fired the gun. She hit Kendall in the right wrist where his Timer was.

He jumped up, letting Jeff go.

"Stop right there!" Maria said. "Stop or I'll shoot again." She wondered if she could shoot again. Probably not. But Kendall didn't know that.

"Put up your hands," Maria ordered.

A few minutes later, Jeff was back on his feet. "OK, Kendall, it's all over for you. Now let's get back to the base camp."

Just then, something flew over Maria's head. It made an ugly buzzing sound.

"What was that?" she asked Jeff. "It looked mean."

"That was one of the insects that killed all the people and animals on this planet," Jeff said.

"Look, there are more of them," Maria said. "Lots more."

The rockslide had set the insects free. They were flying out of holes in the ground.

"Let's get out of here before they kill us, too," Jeff said.

Maria and Jeff were about to press the Return Buttons on their Timers.

Before they could do so, the insects began to circle around them. They started to attack. One

of the insects landed on Kendall's left hand. He couldn't chase it away. It bit him.

He screamed in pain. "Those things can see me!" he yelled. "They are attacking me."

"We have got to get back to the base camp," Jeff said to Maria. "Let's go! Right now!"

"What about Kendall? We can't leave Kendall here," she said. "The insects can see him. Look, the Number Two Button on his Timer is broken. That's why the insects can see him."

"The bullet you fired at him before must have broken the button," Jeff said.

More of the insects landed all over Kendall's body. Some were on his face. Others were on his hands. He screamed over and over again in pain.

"We've got to help him, Jeff," Maria said. "If we don't, those insects will kill him!"

CHAPTER 9

ESCAPE TO THE PRESENT

The insects kept after Kendall. They were also after the people and the animals of Planet X-12. The people who had come to see the rockslide were running away. They were screaming as loud as Kendall was.

The buzzing of the insects was loud. It was almost as loud as the screams of Kendall and the people.

The air was filled with the insects. They went up into the air and then they came down. They landed on the people and the animals. They bit them again and again.

Some of the people were old and could not run fast. The insects caught and killed them.

"Come on!" Maria called to Jeff. "Let's help Kendall!"

She and Jeff slapped at the insects. They killed several of them. But every time they killed one, others took the places of the dead ones. There were too many of them.

"Maria, be careful," Jeff said. "Even if the insects can't see you and me, they can hurt us if they bump into us."

As soon as he had said the words, an insect bumped into him. It bit him on the arm. He slapped it away. It came back. Others also came. They flew around his head.

"Help me!" Kendall yelled. He was covered with insects.

Maria slapped at the insects that were after Kendall. But when she saw that some of them were after Jeff, she went to help him instead.

But they couldn't stop the insects. There were just too many of them. They were tiny but they were very strong. And they did not give up.

"Help me, please!" Kendall called out to Jeff and Maria. *"I don't want to die like this!"*

But Jeff and Maria couldn't help him. They were in as much trouble as he was.

"It's no good," Jeff said at last. "We've got to get out of here fast. If we don't, the insects will kill us."

Maria knew he was right. "But what about Kendall?"

Jeff said, "We can't help him now. It's too late to go back to get another Timer for him. We've got to save each other."

Kendall ran toward the museum. But he didn't get very far. The insects bit him over and over again. Blood ran down his face and into his eyes. He couldn't see. He fell down. He got up and then he fell down again.

At last, he lay still.

"Is he . . . ?" Maria said.

"Yes, he is dead," Jeff said. He slapped an insect that had landed on Maria's neck. "Let's get out of here."

He gave her the new Timer he had brought from the storeroom. She threw her broken one away. She put the new one on her wrist.

"Ready?" Jeff asked.

"Yes," Maria said.

They both pressed the Return Buttons on their Timers.

The cold wind blew around them. The whispering began. Their world turned black.

And then, all at once, they were back at the base camp.

"It's over," Maria said.

"Yes," Jeff said. "It's over."

"Poor Kendall."

"Don't forget that he was going to kill us both."

"I know," Maria said, "But I still feel sorry for him."

"Try to forget about what happened to him."

"I don't think I'll ever be able to forget it."

"I didn't know all that would happen while we were there," Jeff said. "No one was sure just when the insects killed all the people. But now we know when they did. Because we were there and we saw it."

"We should have taken some pictures of it, I suppose," Maria said. "But I'm glad we didn't. It was too sad."

"I didn't like to see that whole world die," Jeff said.

"I didn't either. The people made such beautiful things. I remember a tiny picture I saw there. I saw it just before you came back with the new Timer. I really wanted that picture."

"But you didn't take it, did you?" Jeff asked.

Maria shook her head. "No. But it was so beautiful. I almost wish I had taken it."

"Come with me," Jeff said.

"Where?"

"Come on. I want to show you something."

Jeff led Maria to a large open space of land. It was almost a mile from the base camp.

"Why did you bring me out here?" Maria asked.

Jeff didn't answer. Instead, he began to dig with his hands. He kept at it for a long time.

At last, he found what he had been looking for. "Look here," he said to Maria.

She looked down into the hole that Jeff had made. "Why, those are the jewels that . . ."

"They are the ones that Kendall got away with the first time we met him. He had them on him when the insects killed him."

"Jeff, look! There's the picture I was telling you about."

Jeff picked it up and wiped the dust from it. He handed it to Maria.

"This spot is the one where the museum was three hundred years ago, isn't it?" Maria said.

"Yes, it is," Jeff said. "And this is all that's left of Kendall." He pointed to the pile of human bones that were in the hole.

"Why, he could have found the jewels from the museum here," Maria said. "All he would have had to do was dig for them right here. He

wouldn't have had to go back into the past for them."

"That's right," Jeff said. "But he didn't know that."

"You did, didn't you? You knew it all the time."

"Yes, I did," Jeff said. "I found this spot one day when I was just looking around."

"Can I keep this picture?" Maria asked him.

"I guess so," Jeff told her. "We didn't take it from the past. We took it from the present— from *this* minute in time. So it's yours to keep."

"I'll keep it always," Maria said. "To remember you by. I mean, to help me remember what happened to us."

"I wonder what's going to happen to us next," Jeff said.

Maria saw that he was smiling. When he put his arm around her, she said, "I think I know what will happen to us next."

"I think I do, too," Jeff said. "We will stay together."

"Do you mean as partners?"

"Yes. And maybe some day as much more than partners," he said.

Together they walked back to the base camp.